O-EMkt

Comptroller of the Currency
Administrator of National Banks

# Emerging Market Country Products and Trading Activities

## Comptroller's Handbook

Narrative - December 1995, Procedures - February 1998

**Other Areas of Examination Interest**

# EM Country Products
# and Trading Activities

Table of Contents

## Background

The expectation that emerging market (EM) economies (and the corresponding profit opportunities) will continue to expand at a faster rate than those in developed markets provides business incentive for banks to become active in the EM. Several multinational and regional banks have increased their involvement in EM trading activities over the past few years.

EM trading activities should include the fundamental risk management controls that are part of any properly supervised trading operation. Because of several unique market characteristics, however, the trading of EM products presents heightened risks, as well as additional risks not found in developed market trading activities. This guidance on EM trading and related risk control points describes these particular risks and provides guidelines for controlling subsequent exposures. Although banks are involved in corporate finance activities in EM countries, this booklet only addresses EM trading activities. The control points herein should be recognized by bank management in a formal system of control and reviewed by bank examiners.

As the fundamental business risks inherent in EM activities are similar to those found in traditional trading activities and loan liquification programs, examiners should refer to the *Comptroller's Handbook* section, "Risk Management of Financial Derivatives," for a description of those procedures and controls to be assessed during an examination. The fundamental controls discussed in both this guidance and in Banking Circular 277, "Risk Management of Financial Derivatives," should be part of any properly supervised EM trading operation. A bank's overall risk management system should be commensurate with the level and complexity of its business activity and risk exposure.

In the industry practice, **EM countries** are generally considered to be less developed countries that are not members of the Organization for Economic

Cooperation and Development (OECD)[1] or that have non-investment grade sovereign debt ratings. However, there are exceptions to this general statement; for example, Mexico, widely considered to be an EM country, is a member of the OECD.

Typically, EM countries have lower levels of foreign investment, less efficient financial markets, relatively low gross national product (GNP), non-investment grade or non-rated sovereign debt, and higher inflation and interest rates than OECD counties. However, the degree of economic development among these countries varies. For example, some countries in Africa and central Asia may not use the international capital markets for financing needs as much as certain countries in Latin America or southeast Asia, and may have less-sophisticated market participants, simpler financial products, less-advanced trading systems, and less prudential legal and regulatory oversight than those countries.

Further, a similar discrepancy may exist among OECD members, as some members (e.g., Mexico) are less

---

[1] The OECD was founded in 1961 by Austria, Belgium, Canada, Denmark, France, Germany, Greece, Iceland, Ireland, Italy, Luxembourg, The Netherlands, Norway, Portugal, Spain, Sweden, Switzerland, Turkey, United Kingdom, and the United States. Japan joined in 1964, Finland in 1969, Australia in 1971, New Zealand in 1973, and Mexico in 1994.

developed than other members (e.g., the United States), and exhibit some of the economic and political characteristics outlined above that are generally ascribed to EM countries.

Classification as an EM country, though based on the relative economic, social, and political development of a country, may therefore be somewhat subjective. A country in Latin America, for example, may be considered to be developed relative to a country in Africa, but not relative to one in North America, because it may exhibit certain elements of development that are subsequently offset by country or market characteristics which heighten specific risks.

Some of the EM countries that domicile significant EM products and trading activities are Argentina, Brazil, Chile, Mexico, Morocco, Nigeria, Poland, Russia, and Venezuela.

The current EM environment was largely shaped by the Less Developed Country (LDC) debt crisis in the 1980s, when, for the first time in recent history, many EM countries experienced severe credit and/or liquidity difficulties and left banks with large amounts of problem debt. Much of the debt restructuring activity and economic reform resulting from this crisis has taken place under the auspices of the **Brady Plan,** which was proposed in 1989 by Secretary of the Treasury Nicholas F. Brady.

Under the Brady Plan, certain EM countries, upon committing to specific economic reforms, are assisted in issuing new sovereign debt securities in exchange for rescheduled commercial bank debt. The vast majority of this bank debt has been repackaged in the form of long-term Brady bonds, mostly denominated in U.S. dollars and fully or partially collateralized by U.S. government securities. The potential for large spreads and significant profit opportunities has enticed many investors, including some national banks, to actively trade these instruments.

**Brady bonds** take several forms. The most common bonds include:

- *Par bonds*, which are exchanged for loans at par but carry below-market fixed interest rates. These generally mature 30 years from issuance and are fully collateralized as to principal and partially collateralized as to interest.

- *Discount bonds*, which are exchanged for loans at a discount to face value but carry a market interest rate based on London Interbank Offered Rate (LIBOR). These also tend to mature 30 years from issuance and are fully collateralized as to principal and partially collateralized as to interest.

- *Front-loaded interest reduction bonds* (FLIRB), which are exchanged for loans at par but offer significant interest rate reduction in the bond's early years. The principal is usually not collateralized, but a portion of the interest rate payments is usually collateralized during the fixed rate period.

- *Debt conversion* and *new money bonds* (DCBs and NMBs), which are usually issued together. Loans are exchanged at par into DCBs, conditional upon the commitment of new lending by the creditor in the form of NMBs. DCBs and NMBs are not collateralized, but have shorter average lives than par or discount bonds and carry market interest rates.

- Interest arrears bonds, which allow countries to securitize unpaid interest claims in conjunction with a Brady Plan. They are also known as past due interest (PDI) bonds, eligible interest (EI) bonds, and interest due and unpaid (IDU) bonds. These bonds usually have floating interest rates and are uncollateralized.

Par bonds and discount bonds make up well over half of the volume of the Brady bonds issued. Since the inception of the Brady Plan in 1988, the trading of Brady bonds has become the largest and most liquid segment of the EM debt markets, and now composes over half of all EM debt trading volume.

Increased expectations for improved credit quality and significant profit opportunities have led to substantial growth in the issuance and trading of EM instruments in addition to Brady bonds and the expansion of activities. **EM instruments** now traded include loans, bonds (Brady and other), euronotes, certificates of deposit, commercial paper, local market instruments, and equities. Either a cash instrument or a derivative thereof, such as an option on an EM instrument, may be traded. These instruments may be denominated in U.S. dollars or another currency, and may be collateralized by financial instruments such as U.S. government securities. Because of higher credit, operational, market liquidity, event, and sovereign risks, EM loans and bonds generally trade at a significant discount to par.

**Banking activities** in the EM include the underwriting, distribution and secondary trading of private and public sector loans, bonds, money market instruments and equities. These instruments may be booked as loans or securities in various entities (bank, bank subsidiary, or holding company) for legal and tax purposes and depending on their authority to purchase and hold the particular instrument. Key factors governing the legality of activities, and consequently the determination of entities within a banking organization where these activities are conducted, include significant statutes and regulations, including 12 U.S.C. 24 (seventh), 12 CFR 1, and 12 CFR 11, and whether the activities are conducted domestically or in a foreign country. Regardless of the entity (some banks conduct EM trading activities in their section 20 subsidiaries), the risk management framework should be consistent. Depending on the instrument, banks may execute trades as principal or agent for either their own institution or other market participants. Banks may also function as market makers in foreign markets.

At year end 1994, the Emerging Markets Traders Association (EMTA) reported that the obligations of Argentina, Brazil, Mexico, and Venezuela accounted for over three-quarters of all EM sovereign debt trading. Trading volume in eastern European instruments was the second largest percentage, behind Latin America and followed by Africa and central Asia.

## Unique Aspects of Emerging Markets

A number of unique market characteristics increase certain risks in the EM. The risks most affected by these characteristics are market, credit, and operational risks. Banks must identify the unique attributes that accentuate these risks when evaluating existing or proposed EM strategies and related risk management issues. Some aspects of trading in EM instruments that may set it apart from trading in more developed markets include:

- High market growth and rapid product development.

- High price volatility.

- Less market liquidity.

- Operational complexities.

- Substantial compensation to key EM traders.

- Potential for significant profits.

- Correlated capital flows.

- Greater interconnection of significant risks.

EM countries constitute one of the fastest growing global financial markets. According to EMTA, trading volume in 1994 was greater than that of 1992 and 1993 combined. This growth reflects both the rapid increase in the volume of new debt issuance (due both to recent large Brady reschedulings and new issues in the voluntary markets) and higher turnover among existing debt in the secondary markets. This activity has been driven by accelerating investor demand for EM products. EM investments are considered attractive because they provide the potential for high returns along with global diversification.

Market makers in EM instruments currently include commercial and investment banks, as well as "boutique" operations that specialize in EM trading. The customer base for EM products has expanded well beyond the commercial banking sector to include mutual funds, hedge funds, pension funds, and other large institutional investors. Because of the increasing number of products traded, the growing number of participants, and ongoing attempts by EMTA and other market participants to improve trading and settlement technology and standardize documentation and market trading practices, **the processes of EM trading and settlement continue to change rapidly**. Banks should be encouraged to participate in newly created market processes, such as the EMTA-sponsored electronic matching system (Match-EM) or multilateral and bilateral netting efforts, which serve to reduce risk in EM trading.

EM instruments typically exhibit greater **price volatility** than those in developed markets. This is partially due to trading that is confined to few market participants relative to developed markets, and products may be subject to periodic episodes of significant illiquidity. These liquidity gaps reflect the susceptibility of product values to events such as sudden political changes or financial market disruptions. Most EM countries lack standard trading processes and well-developed legal or regulatory frameworks. The absence of consistent financial accounting and disclosure standards among EM countries and issuers complicates financial analyses and risk measurement, and tends to create greater demand uncertainty compared to more developed markets.

The general lack of standard market practices and developed settlement systems in some EM countries has led to **operations complexity**. For example, although many Brady bond instruments are settled on a delivery versus payment (DVP) basis, thereby reducing settlement risk to a minimum, the trade settlement process for loans and options is manually intensive. There is relatively little automation and standard documentation available in this process. Manual processes generally result in greater error rates and more transaction delays than automated ones, and tend to increase exposures to both pre-settlement and settlement risks.

Although EM **trader compensation** packages may be similar to those in other trading areas, rapid market growth and several recent periods of very favorable trading results have led to unusually high compensation for key EM traders. Institutions entering into or expanding this business have paid significant premiums to attract experienced traders. The intensity of competition has sometimes resulted in entire trading teams being hired away by competing institutions, creating exposure to intellectual risk. Because of this competition for EM traders, some banks may run the risk of overcompensating inexperienced EM traders by offering large signing bonuses or compensation packages in order to expand their EM trading desk.

These unique market aspects accentuate the underlying risks a bank faces when engaging in EM trading activities. Also, adverse events in or changes in investor perceptions of one country have caused market illiquidity and price declines in instruments in seemingly uncorrelated EM countries. Banks need to assess correlation risk and **interconnection risk**, the interrelationship between and among specific counterparties, issuers, instruments, countries, and risks. In evaluating correlation and interconnection risks, banks should consider not only the risks posed by activities or trading in individual EM countries, but also the aggregate risk arising from all EM activities. Therefore, although the following guidance is segmented by the predominant risk factors, the overall risk exposure a bank is willing to undertake should be evaluated on both a country-by-country and aggregate basis.

## Risks Associated with the Emerging Markets

For analysis and discussion purposes, the OCC identifies and assesses risks separately. The Supervision by Risk framework asks examiners to assess nine fundamental risks to an institution. The nine categories of risk for bank supervision are: **Credit, Interest Rate, Liquidity, Price, Foreign Exchange, Transaction, Compliance, Strategic, and Reputation risk.** Those risks that are heightened in EM trading due to the unique market characteristics include Strategic, Credit, Liquidity, Price, Foreign Exchange, Transaction, and Compliance risks. In addition, country exposure (sovereign risk) is a risk specific to EM countries, and should consequently be evaluated by banks trading in these markets.

An effective risk management approach identifies, measures, monitors, controls, and reports risk in all areas relevant to a business or activity. A bank's activity in EM countries and markets should be considered in light of the company's overall risk profile. In conjunction with understanding and managing the primary sources of risk, appropriate research and analysis of the unique aspects of EM trading should be completed before a bank engages in new products or expands activities.

## Board and Senior Management Oversight

The board of directors (board) is ultimately responsible for the safe and sound management of a bank's EM activities. The board, a committee thereof, or appropriate management as designated by the board, should ensure that EM activities are consistent with the overall business strategy of the bank. This entails the development and implementation of a sound risk management framework composed of appropriate written policies and procedures, effective risk measurement and reporting systems, and independent oversight and control processes.

## Strategic Risk

Strategic risk is the risk to earnings or capital arising from adverse business decisions or improper implementation of those decisions. This risk is a function of the compatibility between an organization's strategic goals, the business strategies developed to achieve those goals, the resources deployed against these goals, and the quality of implementation. The resources needed to carry out business strategies are both tangible and intangible. They include communication channels, operating systems, delivery networks, and managerial capacities and capabilities.

The definition of strategic risk focuses on more than an analysis of the written strategic plan. Its focus is on how plans, systems, and implementation affect the franchise value. It also incorporates how management analyzes external factors that impact the strategic direction of the company.

### Strategy and Business Objectives

A bank's EM activities should be consistent with its EM strategy and the overall business objectives endorsed by the board. This strategy may be articulated within policies governing other activities or documented separately. Strategy statements should address the following:

- Scope of activities.

- Objectives for each activity.

- Consistency with bank's overall business strategy.

- Target markets and/or customers.

- Performance expectations and benchmarks.

## Policies and Procedures

Written policies and procedures need to be in place to ensure clear communication regarding the proper identification, measurement, monitoring, and control of risk exposures. Formal policies should address the following:

- Definitions, types, and nature of authorized products and activities.

- Authorities and responsibilities.

- Risk measurement methodology.

- Regular risk position and performance reporting requirements.

- Risk tolerance through comprehensive limits.

- Documentation standards.

- Accounting issues, including taxes.

- Valuation methodologies.

- Legal and regulatory issues.

- Requirements for the development and implementation of operating procedures to guide employees in day-to-day activities.

- A process to approve new products or activities or significant changes to existing products or activities.

Policies and procedures must keep pace with the changing nature of EM products and markets, and significant changes to policies and procedures should be ratified by senior management as they occur. Policies should be endorsed by the board or a committee thereof at least annually.

## Country Exposure

Country exposure (also known as sovereign or cross-border risk) is the risk a bank faces when trading in a jurisdiction outside of its domicile, trading with a counterparty domiciled in another jurisdiction, or trading a product domiciled in a foreign country whose value is directly affected by events in that country. Country risk entails the possibility that the value of an asset may fall, the ability of foreign entities to conduct business may be impeded, or the ability to convert EM currency into U.S. dollars or some other major currency may be precluded (inconvertibility risk), due to a political, economic, or social event (this possibility is also known as "event risk") that is beyond the control of foreign asset owner. Losses may arise from the inability or unwillingness of sovereign borrowers to repay foreign debts, the expropriation or nationalization of property, discriminatory taxation, excessive regulatory changes, social unrest, political instability, or currency inconvertibility.

Country risk is heightened in the EM countries because of political and regulatory uncertainty. In addition, due largely to increasingly sophisticated telecommunication and data processing techniques and the international mobility of liquid capital assets, large capital outflows of short term capital, or "hot money," may further affect the value of assets issued or traded in an EM country. Country risk can consequently affect the value of a country's sovereign debt issues and other assets a bank may hold in that country.

Banks should evaluate individual countries before operating or trading locally, as well as before trading with local EM counterparties or in instruments issued by or domiciled in specific EM countries. Country evaluations should include reviews and analyses of a country's relative political stability, local market size and depth, relevant economic history, and prospective social, economic and political trends.

Factors which should be included in the evaluation of political stability are the type of government, the degree of government stability and/or the likelihood of government change, level of political corruption, stated government objectives and relative ability to implement policies to realize these objectives, level of economic sophistication of government officials, degree of domestic social unrest, and the government's ability to respond to the need for change without causing upheaval.

In addition to internal political structures and market characteristics, external factors, such as a country's reliance on certain imports or exports (and expected trends in these markets) and the potential for external conflicts, should be considered.

When evaluating country risk for sovereign debt, banks should consider sovereign payment history, debt and Inter-agency Country Exposure Review Committee (ICERC) ratings, as well as monetary discipline and resources.

EM country risk assessments may be effected by inherent deficiencies in financial and other data. Access to accurate financial information in EM countries may be limited, and lags in financial reporting may further compound this problem.

In addition to individual country analyses, consideration must also be given to the correlation of EM instruments and activities, as well as to interconnection risk, both on a country-by-country and aggregate basis, as events in one EM country can affect the value of instruments in other EM countries.

Country analyses should be provided regularly to appropriate bank personnel, including line managers. These analyses should also be reviewed periodically by appropriate management for adequacy of information input and analytical accuracy and by senior management to determine significant country trends.

## New Product or Activity Approval

Formal processes need to be in place to ensure that critical issues have been properly addressed and cleared by appropriate parties prior to embarking on a new activity. At a minimum, new products or new activities should be cleared by the business, operations, risk control, accounting, compliance, and legal areas.

Some banks have found that having a process to provide uniform descriptions of products and activities can be an effective risk management tool. The output of this process is a document (product- or activity-specific) that can be used by management and by risk control and audit staff to ensure that risks are being prudently identified, measured, monitored, and controlled. These documents generally include detailed discussions of the risk and control issues outlined above, and should also include a country analysis when new country risk is assumed. Research and related analyses supporting new product or market activities should be appropriately documented.

Plans to enter new markets or to trade new products should consider the cost of establishing appropriate controls, attracting professional staff with the necessary expertise, and/or the cost of training relevant staff. Defining a product as "new" is key to ensuring that variations on existing products receive the proper review and authorization. In defining "new," a bank should consider the effect of changes in its role (e.g., from trader to underwriter), product structure, risk exposures, and legal or regulatory jurisdiction.

## Oversight Mechanisms

As the volume and complexity of certain EM activities make it impractical for senior bank managers and board members to oversee transaction execution and day-to-day management, strong risk control and audit functions need to be in place to ensure compliance with established policies and procedures.

The risk control area (also referred to as "market risk management") should perform independent evaluations of risk levels, their propriety, and the adequacy of risk management processes. These units should also monitor the development and implementation of applicable control policies and risk measurement systems.

Audit coverage should include appropriate appraisals of the soundness and adequacy of accounting, operating, legal, and financial risk controls. Auditors should also test for irregularities and compliance with approved policies and procedures.

Both the risk-control and audit functions should be independent of EM personnel and the risk-taking processes. The frequency of testing by each of these areas should be commensurate with each bank's activities and risk levels. These areas should be performed by professionals who are knowledgeable of the markets and the risks inherent in the activities, as well as the methodologies to identify, measure, monitor, and control exposures. These areas must also possess sufficient stature and authority within the organization to be effective. In some cases, banks may out-source risk control and audit functions to ensure that the professionals performing the work possess sufficient depth of knowledge and experience in all relevant areas of EM trading.

Management must respond promptly to audit and risk control function findings, and the board or a committee thereof should track management's actions to correct any deficiencies.

Although capital requirements should adhere to stipulated levels for trading exposures, the evaluation of capital adequacy should extend beyond the determination of compliance with regulatory capital requirements and should consider the amount of capital needed to support the level and complexity of EM trading activities.

## Risk Limits

The board and senior management should use limits and exposure measurement systems to provide a means of control over aggregate EM exposure and to foster communication of changes in trader activities, market values, and the bank's overall risk profile.

Limits should be directly related to the nature of the bank's business strategies, past and projected performance, adequacy of systems and personnel, and the overall level of earnings or capital the bank chooses to place at risk. Risk limits should facilitate upward communication upon a significant change in trader activities or market movements. Aggregate risk-taking limits should be approved at least annually by the board or a committee thereof, or as market conditions warrant. Senior and line managers should be held accountable for adhering to limits.

## Country Exposure Limits

Country exposure arises primarily from two sources: the country risk arising from the domicile of an issuer of an instrument dealt or held by the bank, and that arising from the domicile of a counterparty to a transaction engaged in by the bank. Notional limits are typically prescribed to address this risk and establish maximum positions to be taken by the bank. Systems that aggregate exposures across portfolios and enable management to monitor the various cross-border positions against established limits should be in place.

Because EM countries and products are often affected by the same market trends and capital flows, country concentrations, and correlations should be considered in setting limits for cross-border exposure. The inherent correlation between these countries and products heightens the level of interconnection risk faced by banks active in them. Banks should consider the interconnected nature of risk in these countries and products when establishing their country exposure and aggregate country exposure limits.

To understand interconnection risk, banks should regularly evaluate market stress situations using scenario or "what if" analyses. Scenario analyses can be an effective tool in bringing new insight into the interconnectedness of risks. It can aid in grasping the total impact of specific events, and it facilitates the evaluation of risk from all angles: Strategic, Credit, Liquidity, Price, Foreign Exchange, and Transaction risks. Finally, and most importantly, scenario analyses helps to ensure against surprises.

## Loss Control Limits

Loss control limits (also referred to as "management action triggers") require a specific management action if a defined level of loss is approached or breached. They help foster communication within a bank. Such limits should be established at levels where management wants to reassess a position or trading strategy. When these limits are breached, management should be consulted to determine whether the position should be maintained, closed out, or additional exposure assumed. Loss control limits are useful in the EM because of periodic illiquidity and rapid market fluctuations. Limits should be in place for both cumulative loss levels as well as the maximum time period that a position with losses may be carried. In some circumstances it may be economically beneficial over the long run to retain positions that are currently experiencing losses (i.e., strategic positioning).

Exposures should be monitored on an ongoing basis relative. Loss control limits should complement maximum exposure controls (e.g., value-at-risk, notional, and tenor limits) and should not be used in isolation.

## Aged or Stale-Dated Inventory Controls

Trading positions need to be regularly reviewed by bank management and the appropriate oversight unit, and stale or non-liquid inventory rigorously evaluated. Time thresholds should be established to trigger inventory evaluation by increasingly higher levels of management and by the independent risk control unit. These controls should motivate traders to trade rather than maintain positions for extended periods of time.

In formulating an exit plan, management should assess the valuation of inventory and consider implementing a formal program of incremental price reductions (i.e., price write-downs) for stale-dated, non-liquid instruments. This will motivate traders to move positions and avoid carrying stale inventory beyond specified holding periods. Price reductions may also be considered for positions where the market moves against existing trader strategies.

Stale-dated inventory can come from the following sources:

*Trading strategies:* Trading inventory may become stale because of adverse price moves inconsistent with the traders' long-term expectations or a general lack of investor interest. Traders should discuss longer-term strategies, where a trader takes a position with the expectation of a credit upgrade at some point in the future, for example, and the positioning of the portfolio with higher levels of trading management. The purpose and rationale behind the strategy and projected time frames should be specified.

*Failed underwritings:* The trading portfolio may periodically house failed underwritings. Following the initial offering period, residual primary issues will be held in the trading portfolio. A failed underwriting may at times result in a loss, which should be allocated internally to the responsible units.

*Transfers from the LDC loan portfolio to the trading portfolio:* Despite the mark-to-market discipline in the trading environment, bank management may be tempted to transfer assets from the LDC loan portfolio to the trading books in order to reduce classified asset totals or avoid affecting the bank's Allowance account. However, all LDC loan portfolio assets should remain in the loan portfolio, be designated "held for sale" and booked at lower of cost or market (LOCOM). Loans that are purchased for trading purposes should be earmarked "held for sale" and marked-to-market. Trading personnel may be used to liquidate efficiently these assets on behalf of the LDC loan portfolio managers. The ICERC transfer risk rating, if any, of the loans, should continue until the assets are sold. Instruments held in a bank's trading account are exempt from the Allocated Transfer Risk Reserve (ATRR) application, as they already should be marked-to-market. Consequently, entries into the trading books should only come from direct underwritings or secondary market purchases.

*Transfers from the trading portfolio to the LDC loan portfolio:* Management should document the need to transfer assets from the trading portfolio into the loan portfolio. Such transfers should generally be discouraged. If a transaction is considered necessary, however, a clear strategy for the asset should be developed, proper credit and trading management approvals obtained, an exception to normal operating procedure noted, and any such transfer should be made only at market value.

## Model Validation

Model validation is the process through which the reasonableness and accuracy of the risk measurement and reporting system is assessed. The frequency and extent of model validation, particularly of the underlying assumptions on which models are based, should be driven by the specific risk exposures created by trading activities, the pace and nature of market changes, and the pace of innovation in measuring and managing risks. Because EM risk measurement models are not standardized and the markets are volatile and relatively less liquid, more frequent validations than those performed for models used in developed market trading activities may be necessary.

Models should be validated by personnel independent of user units prior to implementation, as well as upon significant changes in market conditions or activities. Validation may be performed or supplemented by external auditors or consultants. Model output should also be periodically compared to actual results, and the causes of significant variances analyzed.

## Reporting and Management Information Systems (MIS)

Information that senior management should be receiving includes profit/loss and value-at-risk calculations, statements showing positions relative to loss control or stop loss limits (including management action triggers), positions relative to other established limits, concentrations, and any exceptions to policy. Senior management should also be looking at risk-adjusted returns and progress in meeting strategic objectives. The board should periodically receive information depicting aggregate exposures, trends, and significant policy exceptions. Depending on how trading desks are structured, much of the lower level or more detailed information may not need to be consolidated and reported upwards.

Information systems and resulting management reports need to capture the unique nature and risks of EM activities at both the business unit and consolidated levels. Effective internal reporting will tailor the level of information to the intended audience. More detail is usually provided to line management, with more consolidated information going to senior management or the board.

Reporting systems should facilitate the communication of risk in an efficient manner, both on a regular basis as stipulated by policies and procedures and during times of market stress. Fluid and timely communication between trading, support and risk management units can be enhanced through quality MIS.

Please refer to the "Risk Management for Financial Derivatives" section of the Comptroller's Handbook for a more detailed discussion of MIS.

## Local Activity

Some banks have an on-site presence in EM countries. These branches or subsidiaries are often active in local money market, foreign exchange, and derivatives trading, in addition to loan and bond trading activities.

Trading activities within the EM should be conducted according to applicable U.S. and local legal, regulatory and business standards. In cases where local law is unclear or where an apparent conflict between local and U.S. law exists, legal opinion should be obtained. If standard agreements or documents are not available for transactions, documents used should be reviewed by legal counsel familiar with both the bank's policies and operations as well as local laws and regulations. Adequate oversight mechanisms should ensure local units adhere to bank policies.

## Compensation

Compensation programs should not motivate a trader to take risk that is inconsistent with the bank's risk appetite or with prevailing rules and regulations. Conversely, compensation should be adequate to enable the bank to recruit, develop, and retain qualified staff. In such specialized markets, traders are in high demand and are often recruited in teams. Movement of entire teams can lead to a lack of business continuity, thereby creating problems within a complex and highly specialized market sector and potentially heightening exposure to intellectual risk. Some banks have implemented deferred payment/bonus programs, often referred to as "golden handcuffs," to address these concerns.

When establishing or reviewing compensation programs, as well as when determining specific payments (such as bonuses), senior management should consider: an employee's compliance with bank policies, laws and regulations; performance relative to the bank's stated goals; relative quality of earnings (e.g., risk adjusted returns); competitors' compensation packages for similar responsibilities and performance; an individual's overall performance; and the levels of risk inherent in and caused by relevant trading activities. Banks should also consider contingency plans in order to manage risks effectively in the event that EM traders leave en masse.

# Credit Risk

Credit risk is the risk to earnings or capital of an obligor's failure to meet the terms of any contract with the bank or otherwise fail to perform as agreed. Credit risk arises from all activities where success depends on counterparty, issuer, or borrower performance. It arises any time bank funds are extended, committed, invested, or otherwise exposed through actual or implied contractual agreements, whether reflected on or off the balance sheet.

Credit risk is likely the most recognizable risk associated with banking. This definition, however, encompasses more than the traditional definition associated with lending activities. Credit risk implications will arise in conjunction with a broad range of bank activities, including selecting investment portfolio products, derivatives trading partners, or foreign exchange counterparties. Credit risk also arises due to country exposure, as well as indirectly through guarantor performance.

Assessment of counterparty credit and issuer risks is more difficult in the EM due to limited access to comprehensive and consistently prepared financial information. Because accounting principles in the EM are often underdeveloped, incomplete, or not enforced, there may be problems in valuing certain EM debt issues and in evaluating the financial strength of issuers and counterparties. Accounting standards in these markets can be difficult to follow and may change abruptly.

Given the limitations of available financial information, the high volatility of market prices, and periods of market and product illiquidity, banks must take special precautions to effectively measure and manage their credit risk. A bank's limits, administrative controls, and approval processes should be consistent with those expected in traditional trading and lending activities, while consideration must also be given to the interrelationships of risk elements outlined in this guidance.

## Counterparty Presettlement Risk

The quantification of pre-settlement risk from trades with counterparties should include the current exposure from positively valued positions plus an add-on for potential future exposure. Because of the difficulty in measuring volatility in some EM instruments and the periodic lack of liquidity in these markets, counterparty risk should be measured on a peak exposure basis rather than using an average of the projected exposures. Peak exposure is typically measured as the largest probable price movement or a statistically remote outcome such as a two or three standard deviation price move over the exposure period, whereas the average exposure would be the mean of such probability-weighted outcomes.

Because of the potential illiquidity and increased market volatility (and subsequently greater pre-settlement risk), transactions with extended settlement should be formally tracked and controlled. Personnel independent of the trading unit should periodically evaluate the propriety of pre-settlement risk calculations and the bank should clearly identify and distinguish between transactions that are extended settlement and those that are settled regular way. Regardless of the reason for any delay in the confirmation, assignment or settlement, a bank should manage its counterparty exposure until the trade is settled.

## Settlement Risk

Settlement risk occurs when a bank pays out funds or delivers assets before receiving full performance from a counterparty. This exposure frequently arises in international transactions because of time zone differences. This risk is only present in transactions that do not involve delivery versus payment (DVP). A counterparty's failure to perform may be due to default, operational breakdown, or legal impediments.

Settlement risk is eliminated through DVP clearance. Though most EM bonds (including Brady bonds) are cleared in this manner through the Euroclear or Cedel systems, other EM products, such as restructured loans and options, are not. The propensity for extended settlements for these products is largely due to the manual and paper-intensive nature of the trade processing. Extended settlements may or may not follow a formal settlement calendar and usually entail non-simultaneous deliveries.

Trades reported as in the process of being settled may also allow banks to hide losses as unsettled trades. Counterparty confirms may help determine unsettled trades from failed trades.

When not using DVP, a bank needs to have settlement limits which control the maximum exposure to any counterparty for a given settlement period. Settlement risk limits should be established separately from and in addition to pre-settlement credit limits.

## Issuer Risk

Both the underwriting and secondary trading of an issuer's debt obligations involve the risk that the value of these instruments will drop due to a change in the market's perception of the issuer. Factors that should be considered include: an issuer's credit rating, current and projected earnings, industry trends, and the type, tenor, and size of obligations issued or assets traded. The size of a single issuer, as well as the number and concentration of like issuers, should also be evaluated. Banks involved in debt underwriting should follow existing internal review and due diligence processes.

## Collateralized Trading Lines

When banks provide customers a "line to trade" EM products, higher margin of collateral coverage than that used in traditionally traded products is appropriate. The margin is usually defined as the amount by which the market value of the instruments collateralizing the transaction should exceed the amount lent (for example, credit exposure of $100 may require collateral coverage in an amount equal to $125). This buffer is necessary to normalize the level of security relative to that of more liquid and less price volatile activities.

Initial collateral margins should be based on the volatility of the traded instrument, and trigger points should be established and monitored to ensure additional collateral is requested and received from counterparties on a timely basis. Proper risk evaluation should consider the transaction's term, conditions of the agreement with the counterparty, the underlying product volatility, and the counterparty risk involved.

## Liquidity Risk

Liquidity risk is the risk to earnings or capital from a bank's inability to meet its obligations when they come due, without incurring unacceptable losses. Liquidity risk includes the inability to manage unplanned decreases or changes in funding sources. Risk also arises from the failure to recognize or address changes in market conditions that affect the ability to liquidate assets quickly and with minimal loss in value.

The fluctuation of investor demand for some EM instruments may cause the liquidation of positions to take longer than in more liquid markets, which can diminish an institution's ability to actively manage its risk positions. Illiquid markets may also lead to large bid-offer spreads for EM instruments and sudden swings in the liquidity of other EM instruments and markets. These effects can intensify the price uncertainty for EM instruments.

Banks must consider those elements of the EM that affect investor demand and otherwise affect the ability to liquidate assets in a reasonable time and with minimal loss in value. Some of these elements include EM countries' susceptibility to local political or market events that affect demand for an instrument, as well as local EM instruments' correlation to other EM instruments and market movements in other EM countries.

## Price Risk

Price risk is the risk to earnings or capital arising from changes in the value of portfolios of financial instruments. This risk arises from market-making, dealing, and position-taking activities for interest rate, foreign exchange, equity and commodity markets.

Many banks use the term price risk interchangeably with market risk. This is because price risk focuses on the changes in market factors (e.g., interest rates, market liquidity, volatilities) that affect the value of traded instruments. The primary accounts affected by price risk are those that are revalued for financial presentation (e.g., trading accounts for securities, derivatives, and foreign exchange products).

Several EM characteristics tend to increase exposure to price risk, including periodic market and product illiquidity, heightened country risk, rapid change in the status of counterparties and issuers, local legal and regulatory oversight, and elements of interconnection risk. Processes used to manage price risk in developed market trading activities should be adjusted to address these unique factors.

A bank's systems should be able to quantify price sensitivity by measuring potential changes in market factors, such as interest rates and currency rates. Calculations of exposure, or the value-at-risk, should include the time period it would reasonably take to liquidate or otherwise close out open positions. The time to close out or liquidate positions in liquid markets is frequently one day or less. It is more difficult to determine this time period for EM holdings, however, because liquidity can change rapidly; volatility history is not necessarily a good indicator of the future. The volatility factors and time horizons used in measuring exposure should be documented and supported. As various markets develop depth and trading activity increases, volatility history and trend data should be adjusted accordingly.

Because it is difficult to determine volatilities and holding periods, notional limits governing the volume, tenors, and concentration of types of positions should be used in conjunction with price sensitivity limits to control exposure. Such limits should prescribe the maximum risk level and aggregate country risk limitations. Notional limits are not sufficient on their own because they do not approximate price risk, and should serve to complement and act as a backstop to value-at-risk limits.

## Foreign Exchange Risk

Foreign exchange risk is the risk to earnings or capital arising from movement of foreign exchange rates. This risk refers to cross-border investing and operating activities. Market-making and position-taking in foreign currencies should be captured under price risk.

Foreign exchange risk is also known as translation risk, and it is sometimes captured as a component of price risk. Foreign exchange risk arises from accrual accounts denominated in foreign currency, including loans, bonds and deposits (i.e., cross-border investing). Accounting conventions require periodic revaluation of these accounts at current rates. This revaluation translates the foreign denominated accounts into U.S. dollar terms.

The majority of underwriting and secondary market transactions are based in U.S. dollars or other major currencies. However, some EM instruments are denominated in local currencies. Banks should include such EM exposures under appropriate systems that identify, measure, monitor, and control foreign exchange exposure.

Banks are also expected to follow the procedures outlined in BC-277 and the *Comptroller's Handbook* relating to foreign exchange risk.

# Transaction Risk

Transaction risk is the risk to earnings or capital arising from problems with service or product delivery. This risk is a function of internal controls, information systems, employee integrity, and operating processes. Transaction risk exists in all products and services.

Transaction risk is also referred to as operating or operational risk. It is risk that arises on a daily basis in all banks as transactions are processed. It is a risk that transcends all divisions and products within a bank.

Transaction risk is heightened in the EM due to generally less developed and manually intensive trading and settlement practices, the rapid introduction of products, legal and regulatory changes, and less sophisticated market participants. These characteristics make operations in the EM highly complex.

The degree of sophistication of a bank's operations should be commensurate with the volume and complexity of the bank's EM activity and risk exposure. EM trading requires substantial processing, confirmation, and bookkeeping support. Banks should not participate in the EM without proper systems, operations, and internal controls. Transaction risk should be measured in terms of the adequacy of controls designed to address the processing support areas.

## Separation of Front and Back Office Functions and Responsibilities

The function of the front office, i.e., the trader or risk-taker, is primarily to transact and manage market risk. The function of the back office, i.e., operations, is to process trades and other transactions, record contracts, and reconcile transactions and databases. The operations area should provide the necessary checks to prevent unauthorized trades. A properly functioning back office will help ensure the integrity of the financial information processed by the bank and minimize operational risk.

In some cases, a middle office function has been established to reconcile systems, monitor positions and revenues, and perform other various activities. Several of the banks active in the EM have middle office functions to help provide more timely calculation and verification of profits and losses and to evaluate risk. Both the middle and back office functions should be fully independent of the risk taking, or front office environment, and staffed by appropriately knowledgeable and experienced personnel. Situations, including local market operations, that provide the potential for compromised operational controls and for actions inconsistent with a bank's policies and procedures are unacceptable and may represent unsafe and unsound banking practices.

## Valuation or Repricing of Inputs

The revaluation process is critical to risk monitoring and the accurate computation of profit and loss reporting. Because the EM products or countries tend to have relatively thin markets, quoted or published prices may be scarce. Independent valuation is therefore more difficult.

Market rates used for valuations should be obtained from or confirmed by a person or unit independent of the bank's traders. If any trader prices are used, they should be validated by a separate and appropriate third party or by independently published prices. The bank must ensure a consistent and independent valuation process is in place. For instruments that lack active price quotes, a process whereby prices are derived from similar instruments may be employed by a person or unit independent of the trader. If price quotes are obtained from brokers, more than one price quote should be obtained to ensure objectivity.

The procedures used to revalue a bank's portfolio should be documented, as should any discrepancies in valuation between the traders and the operations unit. Procedures for resolving these discrepancies should also be in place, and significant discrepancies should be reported to senior operations management.

Formal, independent valuations for financial statements and management reporting purposes should be conducted at least monthly.

## Systems

Banks should have systems that gather and communicate necessary information and effectively allow for analysis of this information. Efficient systems provide operations continuity, allowing bank units to fulfill effectively their functions.

A single automated system able to interface all of a bank's systems and handle all trade entry, confirmation, processing and control functions would be preferable, but few banks have such a system. This is particularly true in the EM because of both the manually intensive and the rapidly developing nature of EM products and trading. EM systems, however, should be able to track and/or flag exceptions to policy, procedures, limits, operating guidelines, or controls, and attempts should be made to keep systems current with the EM marketplace. Systems capacity and capability should be commensurate with the extent of a bank's EM business.

## Documentation safeguards

Because EM operations and administrative functions are manually intensive, documentation and paperwork may be voluminous. The absence of complete automation makes documentation complicated, systems have struggled to keep up with business growth. For example, the settlement process, notwithstanding existing DVP mechanisms, is still manually intensive relative to trading in developed markets, as is the manual and paper-intensive transfer of certain debt agreements (both assignable and in bearer form). Draws on nostro amounts, including central bank accounts, and documentation of ownership or transfer can also require much paperwork. Lack of proper or complete documentation can result in inefficient processing, possible legal and trade disputes, and potential trade fails.

Maintaining proper documentation, and ensuring completion and receipt of confirmations, is often a function of operations personnel. Management should ensure operational procedures are in place, including check lists where appropriate, to guide operations personnel regarding documentation requirements and the monitoring and tracking of missing documents. Settlements outstanding for a stated period of time, potential trade fails (due to processing problems), and other processing delays or issues should be tracked. The risk management units, or a similarly designed compliance unit, should periodically review documentation tracking systems for potential backlogs and processing exceptions.

## Telephone Recordings

Because of the possibility of incomplete paper trails and the existence of legal risks in the EM, trading personnel should have recorded phone lines. Recordings will supplement, and in some cases validate, trade documentation, provide evidence in a legal or trade dispute, serve as a control mechanism for traders, and provide an audit trail.

## Compliance Risk

Compliance risk is the risk to earnings or capital arising from violations or non-conformance with laws, rules, regulations, prescribed practices, or ethical standards. The risk also arises in situations where the laws or rules governing certain bank products or activities of the bank's clients may be ambiguous or untested. Compliance risk exposes the institution to fines, civil money penalties, payment of damages, and the voiding of contracts. Compliance risk can lead to a diminished reputation, reduced franchise value, limited business opportunities, lessened expansion potential, and lack of contract enforceability.

Compliance risk is often overlooked as it is blended into operational risk and transaction processing. A portion of the defined risk is sometimes referred to as legal risk. This definition is not limited solely to consumer protection laws. Compliance risk encompasses all laws as well as prudent ethical standards and contractual obligations. It also includes the exposure to litigation from all aspects of banking, traditional and nontraditional.

Ambiguity surrounds many EM laws and regulations because these laws and regulations may be changed suddenly or interpreted in a way that is inconsistent with previous legal or market perceptions. Banks participating in the EM are vulnerable to such unanticipated legal rulings and interpretations of law. This legal and regulatory uncertainty may lead to altered agreements, rules and regulations, contract nullification, fines, civil money penalties and may favor certain local market niches and encourage specific industries or markets. Diligent compliance programs and procedures will help safeguard against these unexpected moves by analyzing, and preparing for, possible alternative legal interpretations.

Compliance programs should ensure compliance with known laws, rules and regulations, and policies and procedures. The compliance structure should be independent from the traders and business units. Responsibilities of the unit should be clearly defined relative to audit, risk control and other oversight mechanisms. Compliance personnel should possess sufficient experience with and knowledge of the EM business activity for which they are responsible. The compliance function should have adequate authority and visibility within the bank to ensure issues are properly addressed.

## Enforceability of Contracts and Legal Capacity of Counterparties

Many times, neither the enforceability of bond and loan trades, assignments, and underwriting contracts, nor the authority of the counterparties to enter into them, has been formally tested in EM jurisdictions. As a result, competent legal counsel should review applicable documents before transactions or contracts are executed with new EM counterparties or for new EM products. Counsel should be familiar with the economic substance of the transaction, the laws of the jurisdictions of the parties and the laws governing the market in which the instrument is being traded or contract executed. Banks should make every effort to ensure that counterparties have the power and authority to enter into trades and agreements and assign loans, and legal counsel should be able to reasonably confirm ownership and assignability.

Nonstandardized contracts, i.e., those that have not been accepted by most market participants or trade organizations like EMTA, should be reviewed by counsel. Similarly, when changes are made to industry accepted contracts, including netting agreements, these changes should be reviewed by counsel. Transaction costs can be lowered by the use of standard industry documents that are widely accepted as enforceable.

## Conflict of Interest

Banks should avoid activities that entail a real or perceived conflict of interest, where one area of a bank may unduly influence the business activities of another. The concept of "Chinese walls" should be extended from other areas in the bank to apply to EM activities, and should, for example, separate traders from credit personnel working with non-public information regarding obligors. Individuals in these areas should not sit on common committees or be in business relationships that involve the discussion of confidential debt restructuring information or other proprietary information.

## Accounting Principles

Accounting procedures for bank records should remain consistent with the Regulatory Accounting Principles (RAP), Generally Accepted Accounting Principles (GAAP), and the strategies and objectives approved by the board. The trading of EM products should be marked-to-market with independent valuations obtained regularly for official reports. The valuation process should be monitored to ensure that valuations remain consistent with market value. Banks should use trade date accounting to record trades.

## General Procedures

The purpose of these procedures is to ensure that banks are identifying, measuring, monitoring, and controlling the risks involved in their emerging market country products and trading activities (EM activities).

These procedures were designed to be comprehensive. In applying these procedures, examiners should exercise their judgment in tailoring the procedures to the specific activities and risks faced by the bank. Current EM dynamics should be considered during examinations.

Objective: To determine the scope of the examination of EM activities.

1. Review OCC documents to identify any previous issues with EM activities that require follow-up.

   ☐ Prior examination reports.
   ☐ Overall summary comments.
   ☐ Working papers from prior examinations.

2. Prepare and submit a request letter to EM management.

3. Review the request information to identify the nature and extent of EM activities and any significant changes since the prior examination.
   Considerations:

   • Management.
   • Activities.
   • Back office operations.
   • Risk measurement.
   • Policies and procedures.
   • Staffing and/or oversight.
   • Country risk reports.
   • Position reports.
   • Credit quality reports.

4. Review reports prepared by internal and external audit, credit review, compliance, risk control or similar functions, along with management responses. Determine the significance of deficiencies and the status of corrective action.

5. Discuss with management the bank's strategies, objectives, and plans regarding EM activities. Determine any internal or external factors that could affect EM activities.

6. Determine key personnel involved in EM activities and their reporting lines.

7. Prioritize issues for the examination, concentrating on profit and loss volatility, market developments, new activities or operations, and weaknesses noted by audit, compliance, risk control, and prior examination reports.

Select steps necessary to meet examination objectives from among the following examination procedures. All steps are seldom required in an examination.

# Quantity of Risk

---

## Conclusion: The quantity of risk is (low, moderate, high).

---

Objective: To determine the quantity of price and foreign exchange risk in EM activities.

1. Review daily, weekly, or monthly risk positions over an extended period of time. Examiners should attempt to obtain data for periods of significant market volatility. Assess the levels of price and foreign exchange risk. Consider:

   - Trading objectives and strategies.
   - The size of positions assumed (e.g., value-at-risk, notional positions).
   - Additional risks resulting from unique market situations and strategies.
   - The adequacy of trading risk management and systems.

2. Review daily, weekly, or monthly profit and loss statements over an extended period of time. Examiners should attempt to obtain data for periods of significant market volatility. Determine if the overall level of profitability is reasonable versus the risks assumed.

Objective: To determine the quantity of credit risk in EM activities.

1. Determine the level of credit risk in the EM portfolio. Consider:

   - Level and trend in credit concentrations, past due loans and problem loans.
   - Quality of counterparty credit exposure.
   - Adequacy of credit review reports.
   - Accuracy of financial information.
   - Issuer risk.
     - Issuer's credit ratings.
     - Current and projected earnings.
     - Industry trends.
     - Type, tenor and size of obligations issued or assets traded.
   - Level of counterparty presettlement risk.
     - Current exposure plus potential future exposure.
     - Peak exposures.
   - Level of counterparty settlement risk.
     - The extent to which products are cleared Delivery Versus Payment (DVP).
     - When not using DVP, whether the bank establishes settlement limits on maximum exposure by counterparty.
   - Collateralized trading lines.

2. Determine the impact of country risk (sovereign risk) on the EM portfolio. Ensure country risk exposure in the EM portfolio is consolidated for reporting purposes. Consider:

   - ICERC ratings.
   - Internal country evaluations.
   - Correlation of EM instruments and activities, as well as interconnection risk.

---

Objective: To determine the quantity of liquidity risk in EM activities.

1.        Determine the impact on liquidity risk from EM activities. Consider:

- The liquidity of products traded.
- The aging of positions and hedges.
- Results of stress testing.

Objective: To determine the quantity of transaction risk in EM activities.

1.        Assess the capacity of the bank's processing and settlement systems and the ability of back office staff to handle present and projected volumes.

2.        Determine if the level of fails or "not through" transactions are reasonable in light of staffing constraints and peak volume periods. Also, review the status of past due loan settlements.

3.        Determine that accounting procedures accurately measure, record, and reflect a bank's positions and exposures and indicate its strategic and investment outlook relative to illiquid and strategic positions.

Objective: To determine the quantity of compliance risk in EM activities.

1.        Determine that management is knowledgeable of foreign laws governing the trading of a particular country's debt and securities.

2.        Review legal documentation exception reports. Evaluate the source, nature, and level of exceptions.

3.        Discuss with management pending litigation or customer complaints lodged against the bank relating to EM activities. Evaluate the source, nature, and level of customer litigation/complaints.

4.        Review the consistency of accounting procedures with the Regulatory Accounting Procedures (RAP) and the strategies and objectives approved by the board.

Objective: To determine the quantity of strategic risk in EM activities.

1.        Discuss with senior management their plans, objectives, and strategies. Consider:

- Risk appetite and strategic mission and consistency with overall business strategy.
- Nature and definition of targeted EM activities, counterparties, customers, products, and markets.
- Current and projected market/product objectives, volumes, and risk measurement methodologies.
- Projected sources of profits/losses and performance benchmarks.
- Distribution network.
- Operational guidelines and systems.

Objective: To determine the quantity of reputation risk in EM activities.

1.        From discussions with management and traders, determine the credit rating and market acceptance of the bank as a counterparty in the markets. If the bank recently experienced a ratings downgrade, ascertain the impact of the credit rating downgrade on their ability to manage risk. Banks may find counterparties less willing to deal with them (e.g., counterparties report they are full up or decline long-dated transactions, calls for

collateral, or early termination).

2.     Determine if there is undue pressure on traders to meet profit goals or incentives for them to take undue risks.

3.     Determine that brokerage fee structures are fair and in line with industry norms.

# Quality of Risk Management

---

## Conclusion: The quality of risk management is (strong, satisfactory, weak).

---

## Policy

Conclusion: The board (has/has not) established appropriate guidelines for conducting EM activities.

Objective: To determine if the board has established effective formal and informal policies governing EM activities.

1. Review and assess policies governing EM activities.
   Considerations:

   - Approved by the board or designated committee.
   - Frequency of updates (e.g., when new products are introduced).
   - Trader limits, position limits and stop-loss limits.
   - Documentation requirements.
   - Types of authorized trading.
   - Underwriting.
   - Approval authorities.
   - Reporting requirements and structures.
   - Accounting guidelines.
   - Operational procedures.
   - Guidelines for trading with affiliate companies and insiders.
   - After-hours or off-premises trading.

2. Review the uniform product description policy. This policy should be a dynamic document that describes/defines:

   - Products and activities.
   - Customer base or target market.
   - Risk, reports, and systems to monitor risk.
   - Formal new product approval process.
   - Accounting procedures.
   - Operational procedures and controls.
   - Legal and regulatory issues.
   - Tax implications.
   - Ongoing update/maintenance.

3. Determine that management has implemented proper policies and procedures on self-dealing by traders. Ensure that this policy states that all trading must be fully disclosed ("sunshine rule") or prohibited.

4. Determine if the bank's conflict of interest policy is sufficient to ensure that the trading unit is separate and distinct from other areas of the bank that may be involved in negotiating debt restructurings or that may have access to information related to such restructurings.

5. Evaluate the bank's policy on selling short. Determine if it requires:

   - Short sales be included in risk/position limits or netted against long positions.

---

- Appropriate oversight functions evaluate the propriety of transactions.
- Transactions be conducted at arms length and receive appropriate management supervision.

6.   Evaluate the bank's policy on selling instruments to private banking clients.

## Processes

Conclusion: Management and the board (have/have not) established effective processes to manage EM activities.

Objective: To determine the adequacy of risk management processes for EM activities.

1.   Evaluate formal approval and limit allocation processes. Assess the soundness of the approval process for limit excesses.
     Considerations:

- How and where limits originate.
- Allocation by region, country, trading unit, and individual traders.

2.   Determine that line management has an adequate risk limit monitoring process.
     Considerations:

- Method for daily reporting of exposures to limits.
- Approval of exceptions to limits.
- Independent verification of information.

3.   Review the bank's new product approval process. Determine if this process involves the input and approval of all necessary risk control and management areas.
     Considerations:

- Business.
- Operations.
- Risk control.
- Accounting.
- Compliance.
- Legal areas.

Objective: To determine the adequacy of processes to manage price risk in EM activities.

1.   Review appropriateness and completeness of the bank's systems and models for measuring and controlling price risk.
     Considerations:

- Do limits and controls qualitatively and quantitatively address all price risk the bank faces, including risk elements and market characteristics that heighten price risk in specific EM instruments?

2.   Determine if stress simulations are periodically conducted to estimate how EM portfolios will perform in unstable markets (e.g., with currency devaluations, foreign investment outflow, recession, social unrest).

3.   Determine the adequacy of the bank's review and control process governing aged inventory.
     Considerations:

- How the bank defines stale inventory.
- How and when the bank prices its inventory.
- Who reviews pricing.
- Who determines at what point stale inventory is assessed; who assesses it; and, if applicable, at what rate and percentage it is written down.
- If a formal policy does not exist, how the bank reviews and records its stale inventory.

Objective: To determine the adequacy of processes to manage credit risk in EM activities.

1.  Evaluate the process in which credit exposure is quantified. Review appropriateness and completeness of the bank's systems and models for measuring and controlling credit risk.
    Considerations:

    - Whether the process considers the instrument's price volatility, product liquidity, and the time required for liquidation.
    - If the process considers the market value of outstanding transactions with a counterparty.

2.  Evaluate the due diligence and credit criteria employed in establishing trading, underwriting, and money market counterparty and issuer lines.
    Considerations:

    - Requirements for financial information, the accuracy and frequency of review, and analyses of the information.
    - Reputation and market perception of counterparties or issuers.
    - Relevant credit ratings.
    - Integration of trading area credit exposures with bank-wide credit exposures to the same or related counterparties.
    - Whether exposure to multiple counterparties and/or issuers is included in one obligor limit.
    - Requirements for loan documentation and requisite research analysis used and recorded in local operations and systems.

3.  Evaluate the management of the credit risk inherent in clearance and settlement of EM loans and debt transactions.
    Considerations:

    - Unusual lags between trade date and the date of confirmation, and whether dealers are subject to broker risk between the time the trade has been executed and confirmed by a clearing agent.
    - Concentration of counterparty risk to clearing agents also acting as principals in a trade.
    - Extended settlement periods.

4.  Determine the adequacy of the bank's evaluation of country risk exposure.
    Considerations:

    - The depth of political, economic and social analyses.
    - The consideration of interconnection risk.
    - The performance of stress tests and scenario analyses.

5.  Evaluate the process for ensuring counterparty and issuer line availability prior to executing transactions.

6.      Determine that the bank has proper controls over margin lending.
Considerations:

- The degree of margin coverage.
- How margin was determined.
- Relevant limits and sublimits.
- Monitoring systems.

Objective: To determine the adequacy of processes to manage liquidity risk in EM activities.

1.      Review the appropriateness and completeness of the bank's systems and models for measuring and controlling liquidity risk.

Objective: To determine the adequacy of processes to manage transaction risk in EM activities.

1.      Obtain a general knowledge of the work flow and job responsibilities within the operations unit. From the review of specific operational areas, evaluate the quality of the overall operational work process. Specifically, determine that:

- Operations personnel report independently from trading staff.
- Front, middle, and back office duties are adequately segregated.
- There is satisfactory transactional documentation to ensure a proper audit trail.
- The staff operates efficiently and operational losses are reasonable.
- Guidelines for local operations are consistent with a bank's operating and risk management guidelines.
- Losses due to administrative error are recorded and administrative problems addressed.
- Daily profit and loss and position data are timely. Traders should have all information prior to commencing trading the next day. If information is not available, ensure that sufficient controls are in place to maintain data and accounting integrity.

2.      Review the discrepancy resolution process. Identify any unusual discrepancies and determine if input is obtained from legal and audit as part of the resolution process.

3.      Determine if there are adequate controls for after hours and off premises trading, and that these controls ensure consistency with the bank's limits, strategic mission, and operational guidelines.

4.      Determine if phone conversations between traders and other dealers are recorded. If so, determine whether the trader can override the system. Determine whether traders maintain blotters or journals that chronologically track trades and keep a running total of positions.

5.      Review the valuation process for all EM traded products with a focus on less liquid instruments. Ensure proper controls exist for product revaluations.
Considerations:

- EM products are marked-to-market for official reports with adequate frequency and market values are obtained independent of the risk-takers.
- All trading centers use common valuation dates and procedures.
- The MTM calculations are computed in accordance with approved policy.
- Price input is consistent and received from a source independent from the trading staff.
- Documentation of price input is maintained.
- Valuation accounting entries are passed to the income accounts at least monthly.

- Traders are unable to change market prices obtained from outside sources.
- Securities sub-ledgers accurately reflect market values obtained from outside sources.

6. Determine if proper controls exist governing the confirmation process.
   Considerations:

   - Are all confirmations handled by operations (not the trading desk)?
   - Are incoming confirms matched/compared to internal documents (e.g., trade tickets, outgoing confirms)?

   - Are signatures on confirmations verified?
   - Are outgoing confirmations sent within 24 hours of the trade?
   - Does operations unit review discrepancies between confirmations and internal trade documents?
   - Are discrepancies reported to front-office traders and supervisors?

7. Determine whether operations perform appropriate reconcilements.
   Considerations:

   - Securities in the custody of others.
   - Correspondent/nostro accounts.

8. Determine if there is an adequate documentation tracking system with follow-up procedures to obtain missing documents.

9. Determine if the back office and LDC debt operations are functionally independent of the trading desk.
   Determine if traders are excluded from:

   - Posting transactions to the general ledger.
   - Revaluing positions for financial reporting purposes.
   - Settling trades and other paying/receiving functions.
   - Reconciling trading and correspondent accounts.
   - Participating in LDC debt renegotiations.

10. Determine if there is adequate control over trade tickets.
    Considerations:

    - Do alterations to trade tickets and other trade documents require the signature of the authorizing party?
    - Do tickets contain all the necessary trade details?

11. Determine if supervisory personnel sign off on accounting reversals to sub-ledgers and trial balances with the reasons properly documented.

12. If separate PC-based systems are used, determine that such systems and any resulting entries are tested and approved by independent parties.

13. Determine if an independent party reviews the volume of business among the bank's brokers to ensure that an over concentration to a single broker or a group of brokers does not exist.

14. Determine if operational requirements are given appropriate attention by senior management.
    Considerations:

- The adequacy of operational planning.
- The degree of interaction between trading and operations management.
- The extent operational constraints restrict the initiation of new activities, or cannot support existing activities.

Objective: To determine the adequacy of processes to manage compliance risk in EM activities.

1. Determine if the board and senior management have established adequate processes for ensuring compliance with applicable laws and regulations, and bank policy.

2. Determine if processes exist to ensure compliance with the legal lending limit for loan trading activity and investment restrictions for bond trading/investment activities.

3. Determine whether proper processes exist for selling instruments to private banking clients. Ensure that no conflicts of prudent person rules appear evident.

4. Determine that legal counsel is reviewing new agreements or provisions for appropriateness, enforceability, and legality. Ensure that legal counsel reviews necessary documents for validation of ownership and assignability.

5. Review the bank's process for ensuring that counterparties have the legal authority to enter into transactions.

6. If the bank engages in "fronting" transactions, either directly or indirectly, determine that proper legal analysis has been conducted for each situation and each country. (Fronting refers to allowing individuals to execute trades through a line of credit and using the bank's settlement process. Certain countries allow only institutional customers to purchase sovereign debt.)

7. Determine if pre-existing bank loans earmarked for sale are retained in the loan portfolio, designated "held for sale" and marked at LOCOM, and that trading personnel only act as agent for the loan personnel to liquidate the assets. Determine whether loans purchased for investment purposes are marked-to-market. Also determine whether the credit rating and ICERC rating, if any, are updated and consistent.

Objective: To determine the adequacy of processes to manage foreign exchange risk in EM activities.

1. If a separate FX desk does not manage FX or translation exposure, ensure that appropriate measurement and controls are in effect at the EM desk.

2. Review the bank's systems to determine the timeliness and completeness of the information used to make cross-border investing and hedging decisions.

Objective: To determine the adequacy of processes to manage strategic risk in EM activities.

1. Evaluate the manner in which trading strategies are formulated, documented, and monitored. Considerations:

- Requirements for approving products, issuers, customers, markets, counterparties, and exposures to them.
- Management's authority and willingness to modify or override trader or front office decisions (via offsetting positions or specific instructions).
- Soundness of overall accounting, operational, legal, and financial risk control functions.
- Modifications for varying market conditions.

- Effective pricing and limit structures.

Objective: To determine the adequacy of processes to manage reputation risk in EM activities.

1.    Ensure that management monitors the entry/exit of major market makers and institutional investors in EM products (e.g., monitoring bid-ask spreads).

# Personnel

Conclusion: The board, management and effected personnel (do/do not) display a fundamental understanding of concepts applicable to EM risks and associated risk management practices.

Objective: Determine if the level and experience of management, trading and operations personnel are appropriate given the complexity of activities and volume, especially during peak or stress periods.

1.    Determine whether management is technically qualified and capable of properly engaging in the EM activities transacted by the bank.
Considerations:

- Brief biographies of managers of units responsible for EM products.
- Job descriptions for key positions.

2.    Review staffing levels, educational background, and work experience of the staff. Determine whether the bank has sufficient and qualified staff to accommodate present and projected volumes and types of EM transactions.

3.    Review the compensation plan and the level of compensation of key employees for reasonableness.
Considerations:

- The compensation package of competitors for similar responsibilities.
- Individual performance.
- Actual performance relative to stated goals.
- Performance relative to other banks.

# Controls

Conclusion: The board and management (have/have not) established appropriate control systems relative to EM activities to ensure compliance with applicable laws and regulations, and safeguard bank assets.

Objective: To determine if the board and management have established effective control systems for the types and levels of risk undertaken in the bank's EM activities.

1.    Obtain and analyze monthly MIS reports used in monitoring the performance of trading desks and assess qualitative and quantitative value. Determine the adequacy of MIS in light of transaction volumes, scope of activities, and value to line and senior management.
Considerations:

- Adequacy of reports for monitoring compliance with limits.
- Adequacy of reports for monitoring aggregate risk exposure by unit and legal entity.
- Frequency and quality of information reported.

- Adequacy of data sources.
- Level of reporting to senior management/board.

2.   Determine if risk-management reporting is adequate and sufficiently independent from the trading desk.
     Considerations:

- Do reports cover transaction volumes, profit/loss, credit risk, price risk, liquidity risk, and other applicable risks?
- Do reports relate risk to capital and/or earnings?
- Do information systems translate technical risk measurements into a format that is easily understood by senior management and the board?

3.   Determine if there is an independent risk oversight unit that monitors trading limits and exposures.

4.   Determine if there is a comprehensive internal/external audit of EM activities.
     Considerations:

- Is the audit frequency appropriate?
- Are audit findings presented to senior management and the board?
- Are systems established to follow-up and ensure accountability for timely implementation of audit recommendations?

5.   Determine if there is an adequate model validation process.
     Considerations:

- Has the bank used professionals for model development and independent validation?
- Are algorithms (yield curve construction, interpolation methods, etc.) documented?
- Are system limitations documented?
- Are models and assumptions reevaluated periodically?

# Conclusion

Objective: To prepare written conclusion comments and communicate findings to management. Review findings with the EIC prior to discussion with management.

1. Provide the EIC with a conclusion memo that sufficiently addresses the quantity of all risks and quality of risk management.

2. Determine the impact on the aggregate and direction of risk assessments for any applicable risks identified by performing the above procedures. Examiners should refer to guidance provided under the OCC's large and community bank risk assessment programs.

   - Risk Categories:             Compliance, Credit, Foreign Currency
     Translation, Interest Rate, Liquidity, Price,            Reputation, Strategic, Transaction
   - Risk Conclusions:     High, Moderate, or Low
   - Risk Direction:           Increasing, Stable, or Decreasing

3. Determine, in consultation with EIC, if the risks identified are significant enough to merit bringing them to the board's attention in the report of examination. If so, prepare items for inclusion under the heading Matters Requiring Board Attention.

   - MRBA should cover practices that:
     - Deviate from sound fundamental principles and are likely to result in financial deterioration if not addressed.
     - Result in substantive noncompliance with laws.
   - MRBA should discuss:
     - Causative factors contributing to the problem.
     - Consequences of inaction.
     - Management's commitment for corrective action.
     - The time frame and person(s) responsible for corrective action.

4. Discuss findings with management including conclusions regarding applicable risks, quality of risk management, aggregate risk, and direction of risk.

5. As appropriate, prepare a brief comment for inclusion in the report of examination. Considerations:

   - Risk levels and affect on bank profitability.
   - Adequacy of policies, processes, personnel and control systems.
   - Any deficiencies reviewed with management and any remedial actions recommended.

6. Prepare a memorandum or update the work program with any information that will facilitate future examinations. Considerations:

   - Soundness of objectives, strategies, policies, and procedures.
   - Levels of risk outstanding.
   - Effectiveness of risk management, limits, MIS, and management/board supervision.
   - Adequacy of personnel, operations, and internal controls.
   - Quality of earnings and the overall risk versus reward relationship.
   - Other significant matters.

7.    Update the OCC database and any applicable report of examination schedules or tables.

8.    Organize and reference working papers in accordance with OCC guidance.

## Request Letter

The following provides guidance to the examiner preparing a request letter before an on-site examination of emerging markets products and activities. Consistent with OCC policy, the examiner should use existing bank management reports whenever possible and keep to a minimum reports that bank management must prepare specifically for the examiner. Also, examiners should request only the items in this list that apply to the risks to be evaluated during the examination.

_____ 1. Policies and procedures applicable to EM activity.

_____ 2. Business plan or strategic plan for EM activity.

_____ 3. Organizational chart and position descriptions of trading and operations departments.

_____ 4. A description of the risk measurement system.

_____ 5. Complete listing of trading limits and controls applicable to the department and individual traders.

_____ 6. Description of the new product or uniform product description process.

_____ 7. Reports or summaries that include EM risk provided to the board, or a committee thereof.

_____ 8. Minutes of applicable committees meetings.

_____ 9. Copy of monthly, weekly, and daily management reports, along with a distribution list.

_____ 10. Inventory of all positions by trader and trading units, indicating those positions which caused significant trading profits and losses.

_____ 11. Monthly profit and loss summaries that show daily results by trader and trading units.

_____ 12. Portfolio aging report.

_____ 13. Copy of most recent revaluation documentation.

_____ 14. List of counterparty credit exposure.

_____ 15. Monthly and year-to-date revenue and expense reports by instrument, trader, and trading units.

_____ 16. List of extended settlement contracts.

_____ 17. List of trading systems.

_____ 18. Resumes of managers and traders.

_____ 19.  Summary of compensation programs.

_____ 20.  Actual compensation paid to senior managers and line officers for last fiscal period.

_____ 21.  List of individuals who voluntarily or involuntarily left the employment of the department over the last year with a brief description of the reason for leaving.

_____ 22.  Copies of reports prepared by internal and external audit, credit review, compliance, risk control or similar functions, along with management responses.

_____ 23.  Copies of any policy exceptions recorded between exams.

## OCC Issuances

Advisory Letter 94-2, Purchases of Structured Notes
Advisory Letter 95-1, Interest Rate Risk
Banking Circular 277, Risk Management of Financial Derivatives
OCC Bulletin 94-32, Risk-Based Capital Model
OCC Bulletin 95-28, Interest Rate Risk Management—Questions
and Answers

## Laws

Financial Institutions Reform, Recovery, and Enforcement Act of
1989

## Regulations

12 CFR 3
12 CFR 211

www.ingramcontent.com/pod-product-compliance
Lightning Source LLC
Chambersburg PA
CBHW080339290526
45790CB00010B/3763